YOU CAN DRAW
DRAGONS, UNICORNS,
AND OTHER
MAGICAL CREATURES

by Mattia Cerato

PICTURE WINDOW BOOKS
a capstone imprint

MATERIALS

Before you start your amazing drawings, there are a few things you'll need.

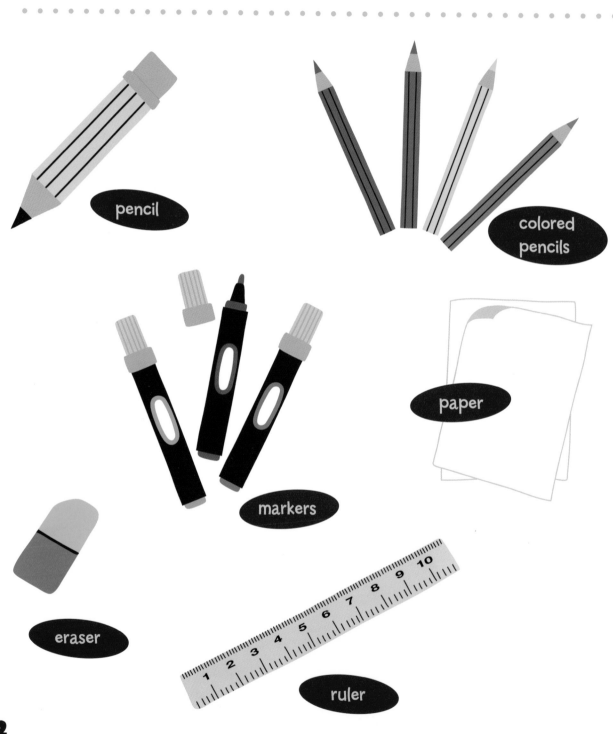

pencil

colored pencils

paper

markers

eraser

ruler

SHAPES

Drawing can be easy! In fact, if you can draw these simple letters, numbers, shapes, and lines, YOU CAN DRAW anything in this book.

letters

DSLU
VZ

numbers

123

shapes

lines

OGRE

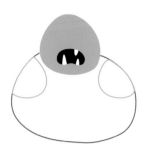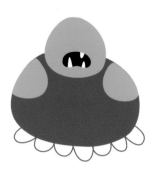

UNICORN

ELF

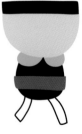

4

GOBLIN

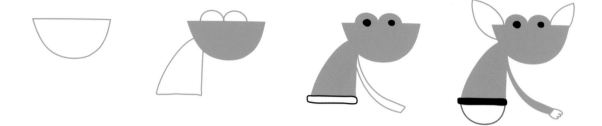

FAUN

DWARF

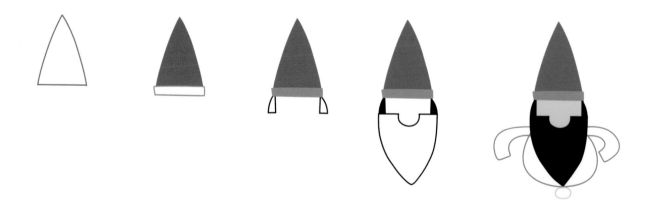

6

Now try this!

WIZARD

TROLL

CENTAUR

  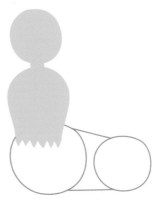 

9

DRAGON

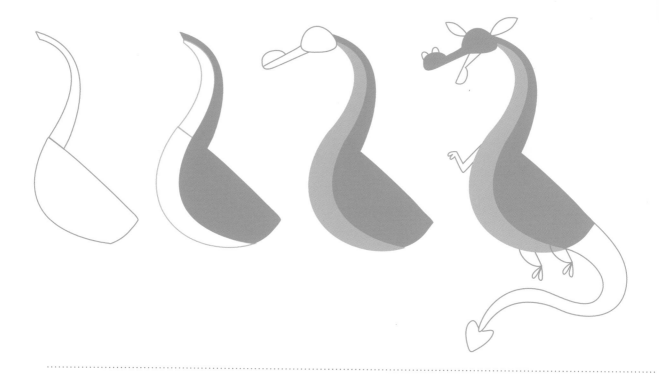

GIANT

GRIFFON

BABY DRAGON

PEGASUS

MERMAID

THREE-HEADED SNAKE

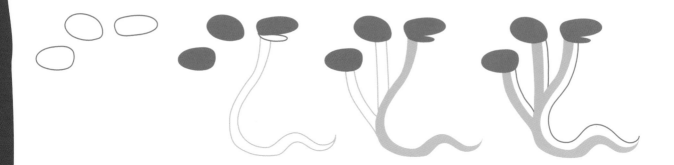

WITCH

CYCLOPS

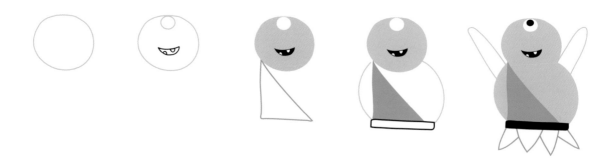

MERMAN

MEDUSA

CERBERUS

Now try this!

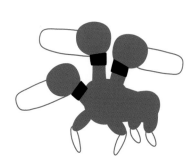

MINOTAUR

PHOENIX

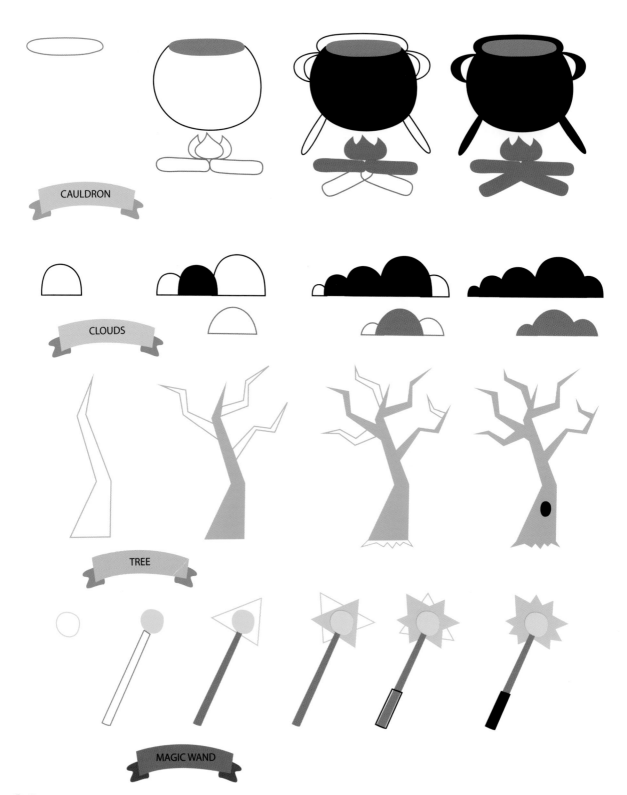

CAULDRON

CLOUDS

TREE

MAGIC WAND

CASTLE

MOUNTAINS

HILLS

CAVE

LIGHTNING BOLT

22

23

All books published by Picture Window Books
are manufactured with paper containing at least
10 percent post-consumer waste.

Library of Congress Cataloging-in-Publication Data
Cerato, Mattia.
  You can draw dragons, unicorns, and other magical creatures /
by Mattia Cerato.
    p. cm. — (You can draw)
  ISBN 978-1-4048-6809-0 (library binding)
  1. Dragons in art—Juvenile literature. 2. Unicorns in art—Juvenile
literature. 3. Drawing—Technique—Juvenile literature. I. Title.
II. Series.
NC825.D72C47 2012
  743'.87—dc22   2011006998

Printed in the United States of America in North Mankato, Minnesota.
022012   006603R

Picture Window Books
1710 Roe Crest Drive
North Mankato, MN 56003
www.capstonepub.com

Editor: Shelly Lyons
Designer: Matt Bruning
Art Director: Nathan Gassman
Production Specialist: Sarah Bennett
The illustrations in this book were created digitally.

Internet Sites •

FactHound offers a safe, fun way to find Internet sites related to this book.
All of the sites on FactHound have been researched by our staff.

Here's all you do:

Visit *www.facthound.com*

Type in this code: 9781404868090

Super-cool stuff! Check out projects, games and lots more at
www.capstonekids.com

Look for all the books in the **You Can Draw** series: